THE STORM THAT STOPPED

PACKED WITH PUZZLES AND ACTIVITIES!

Art and activity book

Finish the picture by
drawing lots and lots of
people listening to Jesus!

the good book
for children

The Storm that Stopped Art and Activity Book
© The Good Book Company 2017. Reprinted 2018.

'The Good Book For Children' is an imprint of The Good Book Company Ltd
Tel: 0333 123 0880 International: +44 (0) 208 942 0880 Email: info@thegoodbook.co.uk

UK: www.thegoodbook.co.uk North America: www.thegoodbook.com
Australia: www.thegoodbook.com.au New Zealand: www.thegoodbook.co.nz

Design and illustration by André Parker, based on original illustrations by Catalina Echeverri

ISBN: 9781784981778 | Printed in India

One day, long ago,
    Jesus was teaching people by the sea.

Soon, some more people arrived.
    Then others. Then more, AND MORE
– until there were people everywhere!

No one could see Jesus and no one
could hear Jesus.

Can you draw some of
the things Jesus was
teaching about?

So Jesus asked his friends, the disciples,
to push their boat out onto the water.

Now the people could all see and hear Jesus
as he told them all about God.

When he finished teaching the people,
   Jesus said to his friends:

LET'S GO OVER TO THE OTHER SIDE OF THE SEA.

Jesus had finished teaching the crowd,
and now he had something to teach his friends
— but they didn't know it yet...

Draw Jesus' friends
in the boat!

So they all jumped in the boat with him
and set sail across the sea...

Wordsearch

h	K	i	g	b	h	s	a	i	l	s	a	j	h	u
n	e	l	d	h	u	i	t	r	z	a	q	b	r	y
e	K	i	j	i	f	t	r	h	b	c	r	o	w	d
l	w	r	m	a	s	a	e	s	l	K	m	a	n	v
e	h	e	d	e	e	c	s	b	g	a	e	t	a	t
a	e	o	i	h	a	s	i	a	d	l	l	v	g	b
r	g	z	d	a	k	e	s	p	o	r	s	u	h	k
n	o	i	i	i	d	u	i	g	l	y	i	r	a	a
l	k	h	u	r	s	p	e	l	e	e	i	d	p	w
a	l	x	a	e	o	c	K	s	i	m	s	c	p	n
z	j	g	j	n	s	u	i	s	e	e	b	m	y	o
s	i	o	p	h	p	b	w	p	h	a	a	s	a	w
e	f	r	i	e	n	d	s	g	t	t	i	c	i	n
z	o	y	e	t	h	e	r	l	y	e	f	g	i	l
s	u	e	g	t	e	a	c	h	i	n	g	s	f	a

☐ Jesus   ☐ crowd   ☐ friends

☐ boat   ☐ learn   ☐ happy

☐ teaching   ☐ see   ☐ sail

☐ disciples   ☐ hear   ☐ sea

Jesus was so tired — he'd been
   teaching the people all day —
so he lay down in the back of the boat
   and fell fast asleep.

Fill this space with
bubbles and seaweed!

Asleep in the boat

Draw some fish
swimming here

How about
a turtle or an
octopus?

It was a quiet evening.
　　The water gently lapped against the boat,
and the sun slowly set in the sky.

Spot the difference

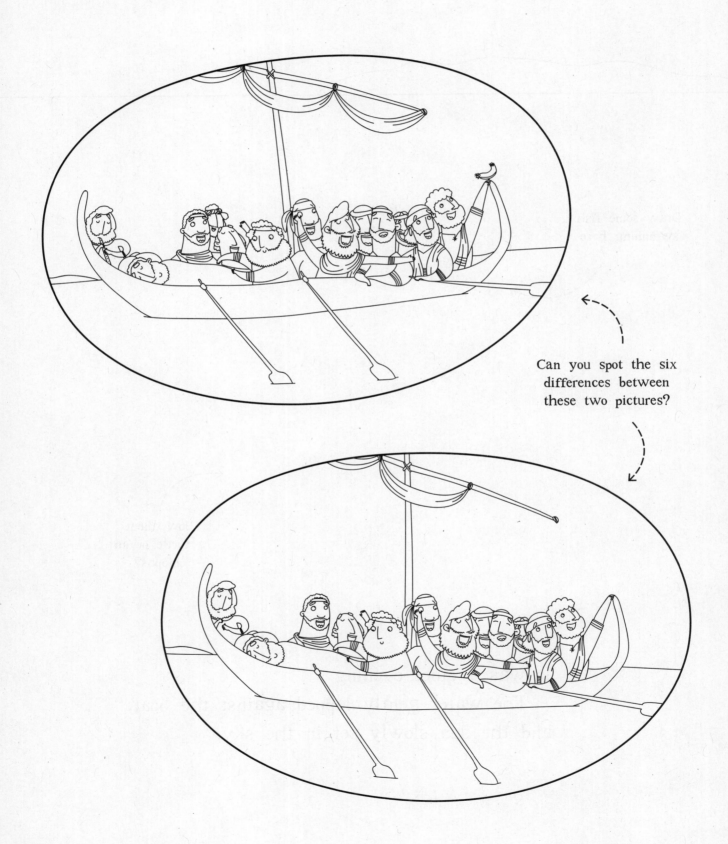

Can you spot the six differences between these two pictures?

Storm!

All of a sudden they were in the middle of the biggest, loudest, scariest, most GINORMOUS storm you could imagine!

And Jesus was asleep!

Wordsearch

h	k	i	g	b	h	r	g	s	s	s	a	j	p	u
n	e	l	a	g	u	t	s	p	l	a	s	h	e	y
e	k	i	j	s	f	t	l	h	b	r	i	v	a	r
u	s	r	n	a	l	p	e	s	l	k	m	d	c	v
y	h	i	d	e	s	e	s	b	g	a	a	o	e	t
h	a	o	i	n	a	e	e	a	d	l	u	m	f	b
r	g	z	s	a	k	e	z	p	o	w	l	u	u	k
y	o	i	i	b	d	d	i	g	l	a	s	r	l	a
l	k	h	u	b	i	p	e	l	c	v	h	d	k	w
a	l	x	a	a	o	u	k	s	i	e	o	c	u	n
z	t	i	r	e	d	u	f	s	z	s	u	m	h	h
s	i	f	p	h	p	b	w	r	h	f	t	d	l	u
e	a	r	b	m	l	o	r	g	j	t	i	c	i	g
t	a	g	e	v	h	e	s	c	a	r	y	g	i	e
s	u	e	g	s	t	o	r	m	e	x	i	f	f	a

- [ ] tired
- [ ] asleep
- [ ] calm
- [ ] peaceful
- [ ] storm
- [ ] rain
- [ ] waves
- [ ] scary
- [ ] shout
- [ ] afraid
- [ ] huge
- [ ] splash

Complete the faces

How were Jesus' friends feeling in the storm? Draw some scared and worried faces:

Jesus stood up in the boat.
The wind was still blowing.

He spoke to the storm.
To the wind. And to the waves.

SPLASH!
SPLOOSH!
QUIET!
BE STILL!
SPLASH!
CRASH!

All calm

Just three little words...
and the storm stopped.

Right away, at that very moment,
the sea was quiet, still and calm.

Then Jesus looked
at his friends.

But they were terrified.
And they asked each other:

Wordsearch

h	a	d	i	s	c	i	p	l	e	s	a	j	h	u
s	p	o	k	e	g	i	s	r	z	i	k	e	b	y
r	k	a	j	u	e	t	r	a	b	n	e	v	e	m
o	w	r	r	t	g	g	e	s	r	k	f	d	l	v
s	h	e	i	a	p	b	o	s	t	i	l	l	i	t
s	e	v	i	n	s	e	k	m	d	n	h	p	e	b
p	s	z	c	a	k	i	d	o	b	g	s	e	v	k
i	t	i	i	u	m	n	i	g	l	y	i	n	e	a
l	o	h	u	a	i	a	e	l	e	k	i	d	t	w
a	p	x	r	w	x	t	z	s	i	s	u	c	d	n
z	p	h	f	p	a	b	b	e	y	t	a	o	h	q
s	e	o	p	h	g	t	w	i	d	f	g	r	n	u
j	d	s	u	s	l	y	e	g	n	t	i	c	a	i
t	e	f	r	i	e	n	d	r	y	u	f	g	c	e
s	u	e	g	t	e	y	m	f	o	t	r	u	s	t

- ☐ wind
- ☐ water
- ☐ sinking
- ☐ spoke
- ☐ quiet
- ☐ still
- ☐ disciples
- ☐ amazed
- ☐ stopped
- ☐ trust
- ☐ believe
- ☐ God

Match the shadows

These people are all from the story – can you help match them to their shadows?

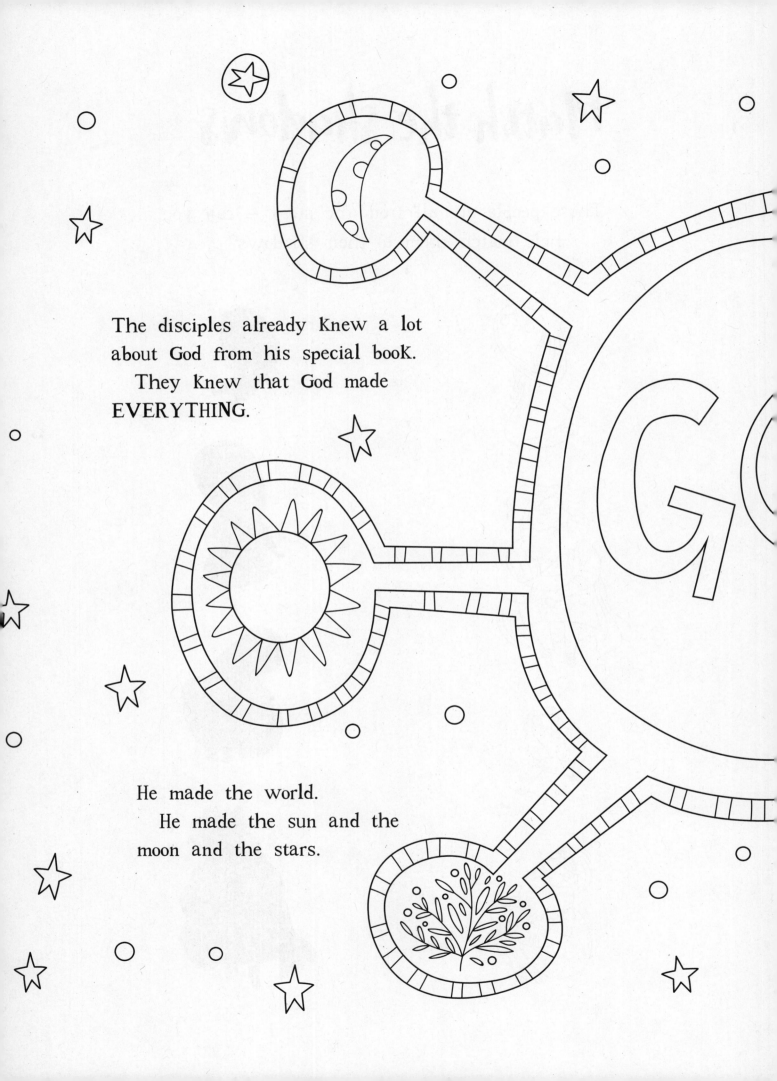

The disciples already knew a lot about God from his special book. They knew that God made **EVERYTHING**.

He made the world. He made the sun and the moon and the stars.

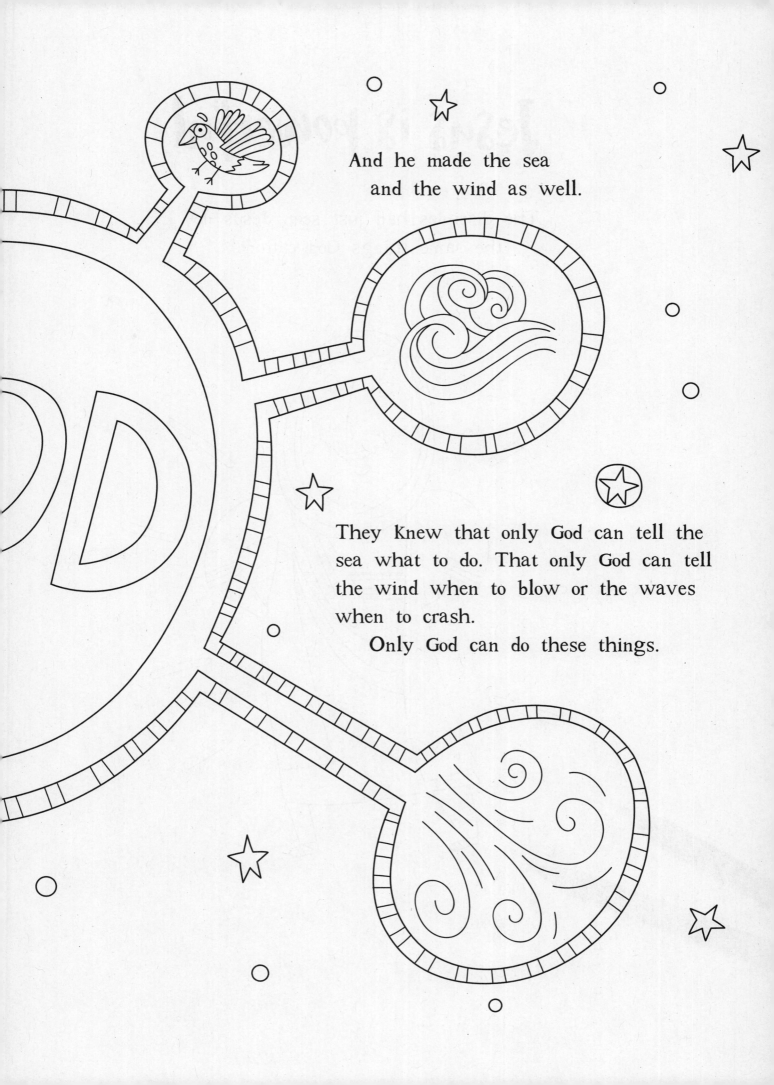

And he made the sea
and the wind as well.

They knew that only God can tell the
sea what to do. That only God can tell
the wind when to blow or the waves
when to crash.

Only God can do these things.

Jesus is powerful

The disciples had just seen Jesus do
the same things God can do!

Use these frames to
draw lots of things that
Jesus has made!

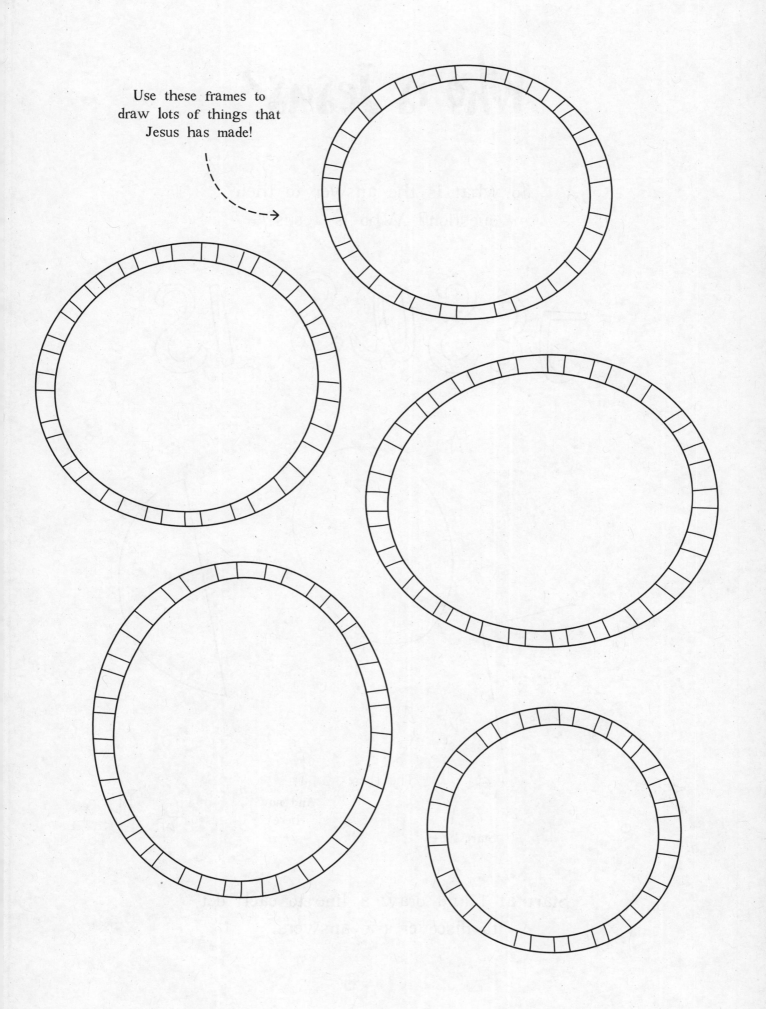

Who is Jesus?

So what is the answer to their question? Who is Jesus?

Start at 1 and draw a line to each dot
to discover the answer...

Going home maze

Can you help the disciples
get back to the beach?

Answers

Wordsearch 1

h	K	i	g	b	h	s	a	i	l	s	a	j	h	u
n	e	l	d	h	u	i	t	r	z	a	q	b	r	y
e	K	i	j	i	f	t	r	h	b	c	r	o	w	d
l	w	r	m	a	s	a	e	s	l	K	m	a	n	v
e	h	e	d	e	e	c	s	b	g	a	e	t	a	t
a	e	o	i	h	a	s	i	a	d	l	l	v	g	b
r	g	z	d	a	K	e	s	p	o	r	s	u	h	K
n	o	i	i	i	d	u	i	g	l	y	i	r	a	a
l	K	h	u	r	s	p	e	l	e	e	i	d	p	w
a	l	x	a	e	o	c	K	s	i	m	s	c	p	n
z	j	g	j	n	s	u	i	s	e	e	b	m	y	o
s	i	o	p	h	p	b	w	p	h	a	a	s	a	w
e	f	r	i	e	n	d	s	g	t	t	i	c	i	n
z	o	y	e	t	h	e	r	l	y	e	f	g	i	l
s	u	e	g	t	e	a	c	h	i	n	g	s	f	a

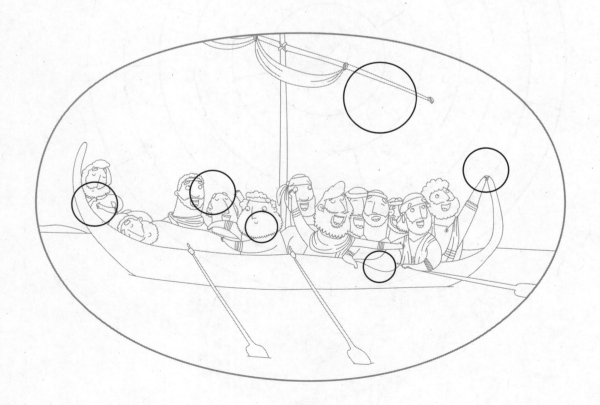

Wordsearch 2

h	K	i	g	b	h	r	g	s	s	s	a	j	p	u
n	e	l	a	g	u	t	s	p	l	a	s	h	e	y
e	K	i	j	s	f	t	l	h	b	r	i	v	a	r
u	s	r	n	a	l	p	e	s	l	K	m	d	c	t
y	h	i	d	e	s	e	s	b	g	a	a	o	e	b
h	a	o	i	n	a	e	e	a	d	l	u	m	f	b
r	g	z	s	a	k	e	z	p	o	w	l	u	u	K
y	o	i	i	b	d	d	i	g	l	a	s	r	l	a
l	K	h	u	b	i	p	e	l	c	v	h	d	K	w
a	l	x	a	a	o	u	K	s	i	e	o	c	u	n
z	t	i	r	e	d	u	f	s	z	s	u	m	h	h
s	i	f	p	h	p	b	w	r	h	f	t	d	l	u
e	a	r	b	m	l	o	r	g	j	t	i	c	i	g
t	a	g	e	v	h	e	s	c	a	r	y	g	i	e
s	u	e	g	s	t	o	r	m	e	x	i	f	f	a

Match the shadows

Wordsearch 3

h	a	d	i	s	c	i	p	l	e	s	a	j	h	u
s	p	o	K	e	g	i	s	r	z	i	K	e	b	y
r	k	a	j	u	e	t	r	a	b	n	e	v	e	m
o	w	r	r	t	g	g	e	s	r	K	f	d	l	v
s	h	e	i	a	p	b	o	s	t	i	l	l	i	t
s	e	v	i	n	s	e	K	m	d	n	h	p	e	b
p	s	z	c	a	K	i	d	o	b	g	s	e	v	K
i	t	i	i	u	m	n	i	g	l	y	i	n	e	a
l	o	h	u	a	i	a	e	l	e	K	i	d	t	w
a	p	x	r	w	x	t	z	s	i	s	u	c	d	n
z	p	h	f	p	a	b	b	e	y	t	a	o	h	q
s	e	o	p	h	g	t	w	i	d	f	g	r	n	u
j	d	s	u	s	l	y	e	g	n	t	i	c	a	i
t	e	f	r	i	e	n	d	r	y	u	f	g	c	e
s	u	e	g	t	e	y	m	f	o	t	r	u	s	t

Going home maze

Now read the book!

If you enjoyed this activity book, read the full story in "The Storm that Stopped".

Other books available in the award-winning "Tales that Tell the Truth" series:

An exciting journey leads to an unexpected twist in "The One O'Clock Miracle!"

Meet God's Rescuing King in "The Christmas Promise"

CHILDREN'S BOOK OF THE YEAR —2016— SPEAKING VOLUMES CHRISTIAN BOOK AWARDS

Discover the story of the whole Bible in "The Garden, the Curtain and the Cross"

Learn how God made people to enjoy being delightfully different but all part of the same family in "God's Very Good Idea"

www.thegoodbook.co.uk
www.thegoodbook.com

This true story about Jesus
comes from the Bible. You will
find it in Mark 4 v 35-41.